I0494705

ink

a photo series

A tattoo is a wound, where ink is injected into the dermis, or second layer of the skin, to create a design. Throughout history, tattooing has been used as therapeutic treatments, symbols of status, signs of religious beliefs, personal adornments, declarations of love, forms of identification, and even a form of punishment. The evolution and acceptance of tattoos and body art has a long and complex story.

Today, tattoos have become an exceedingly popular form of self-expression. Everyone from your neighbor to your grandmother is likely to be tattooed.

This series explores the diversity of tattooed people: the souls behind the skin. From roller derby girls to accountants, tattoos are everywhere. They are now widely accepted as a legitimate art form and not a declaration of unruliness.

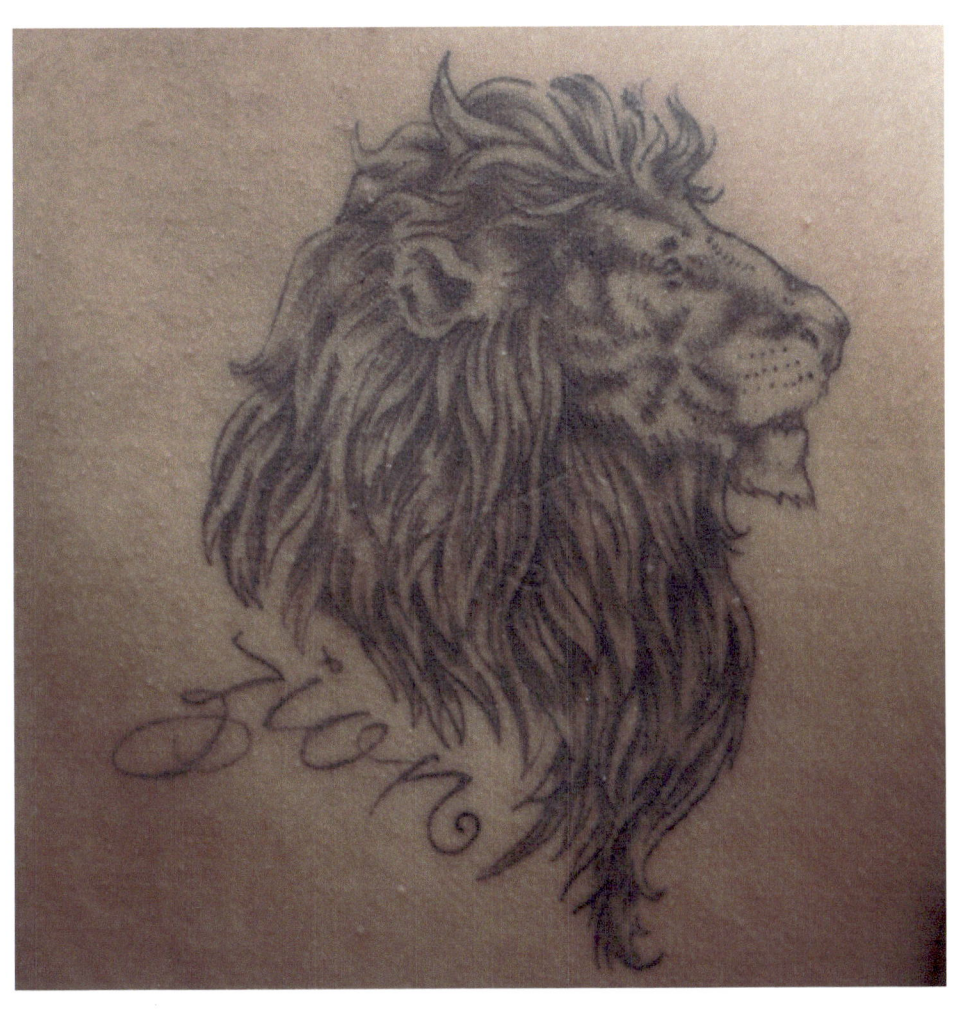

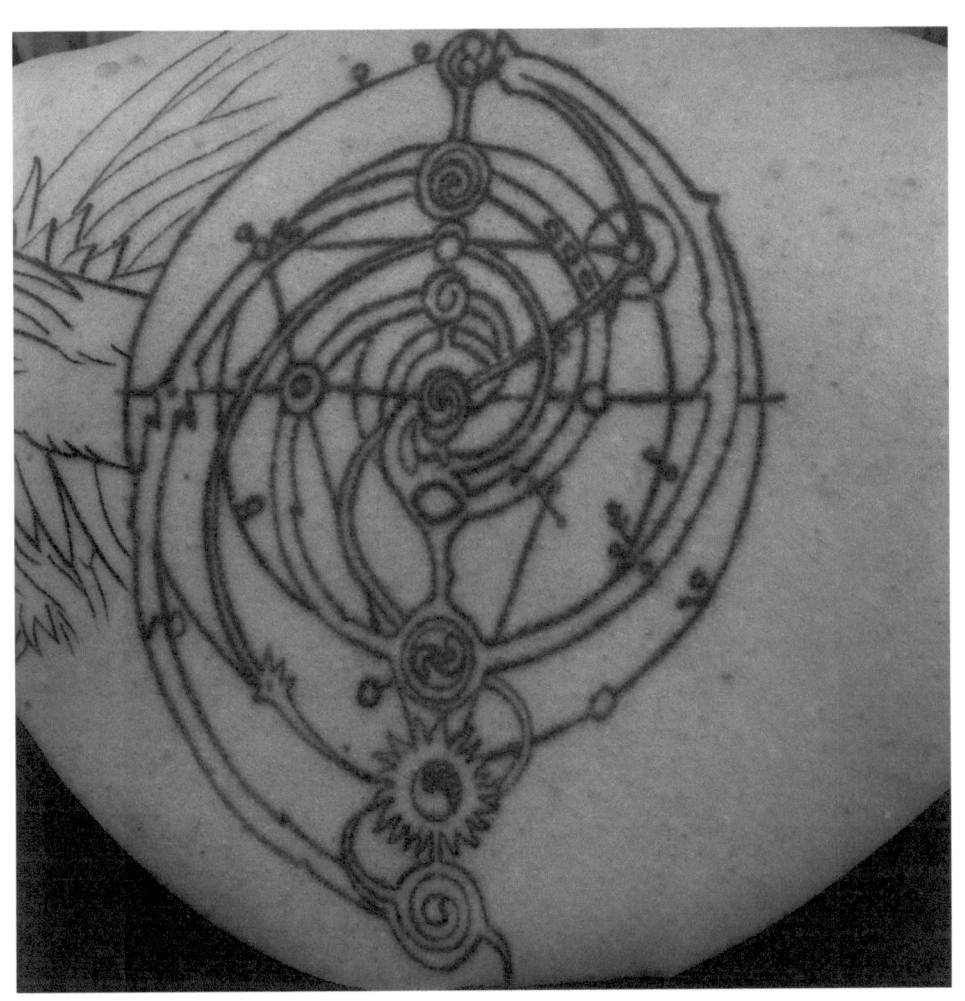

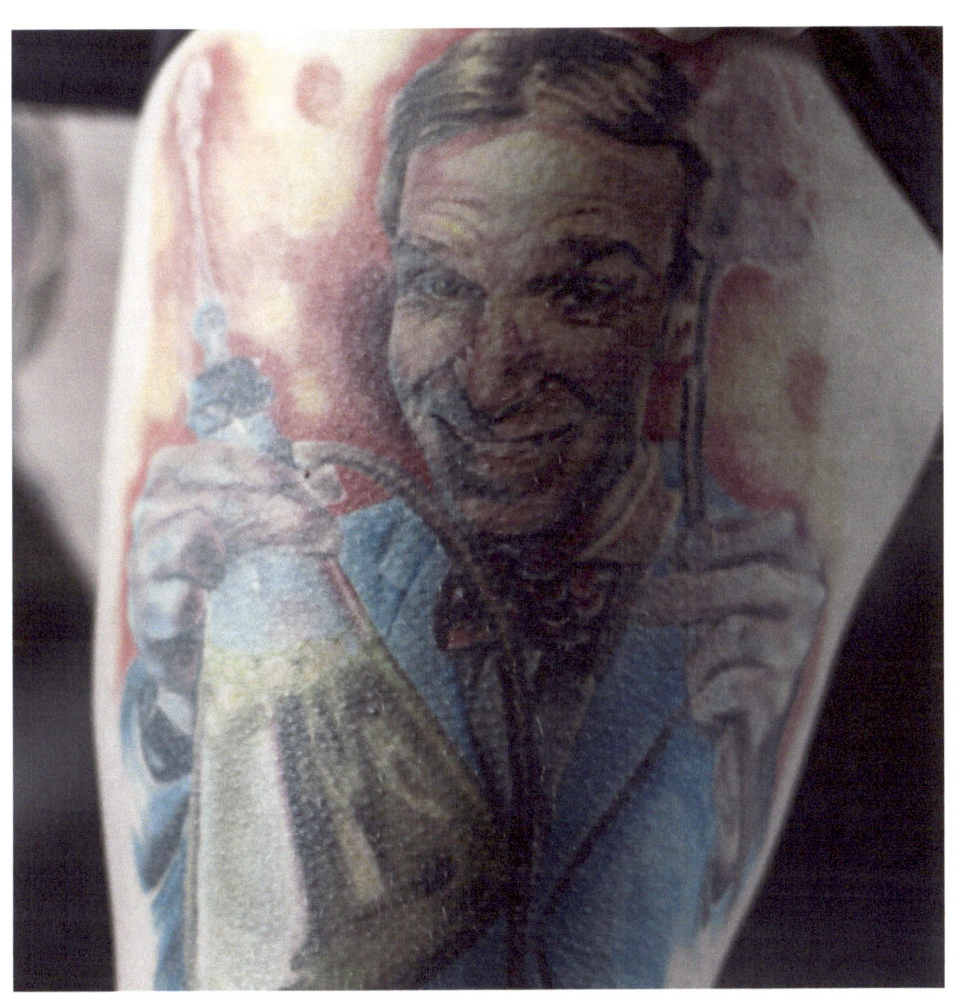

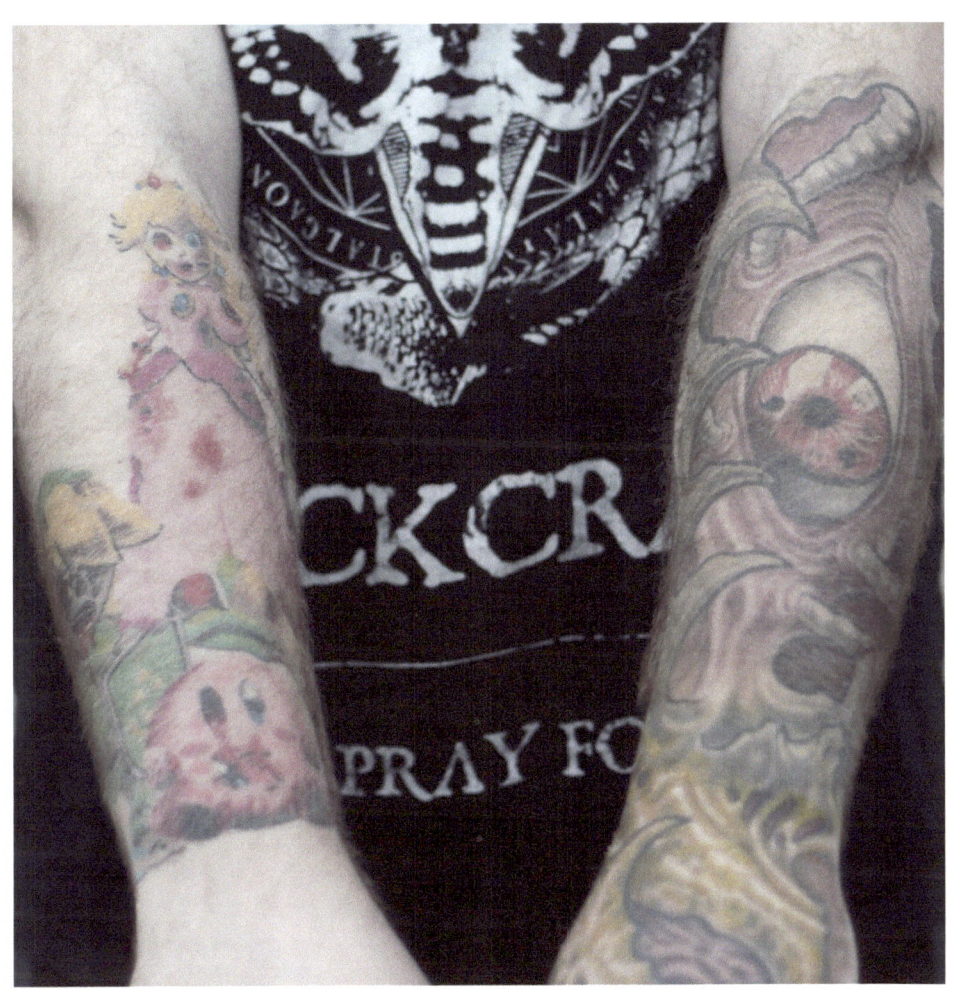

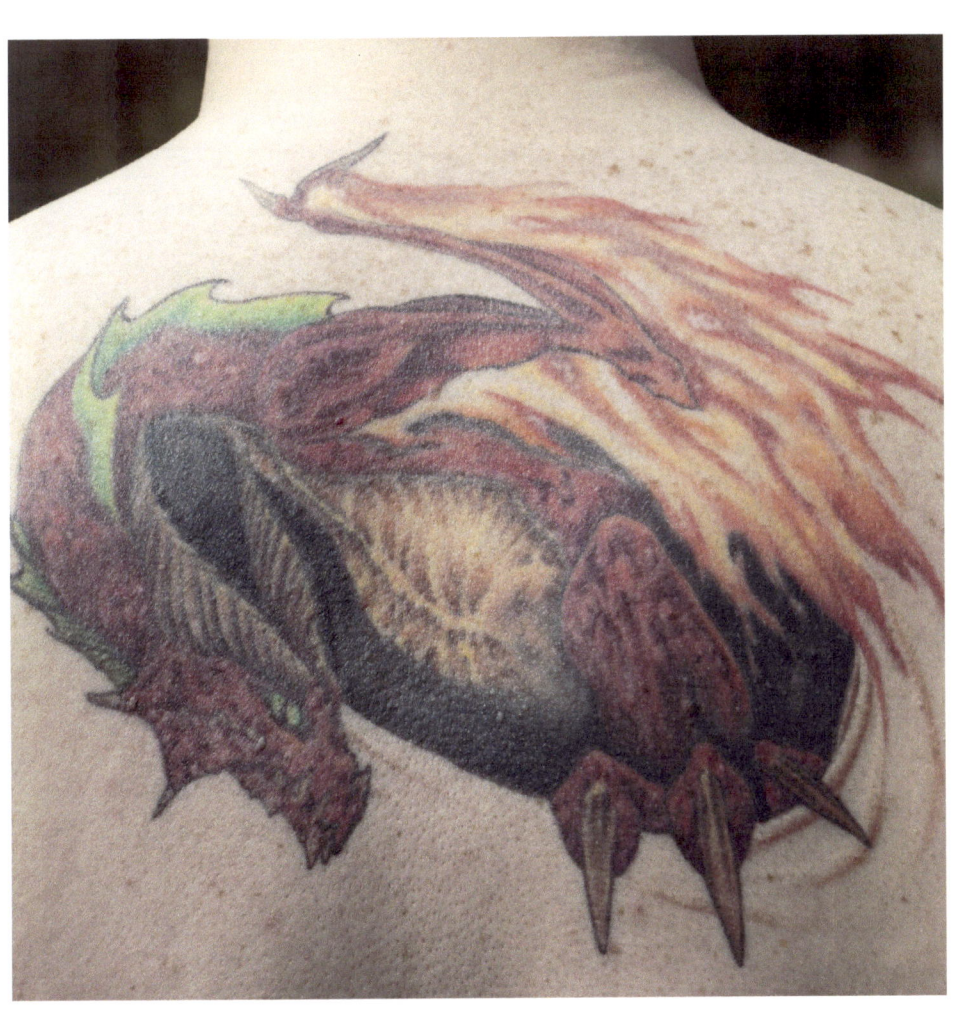

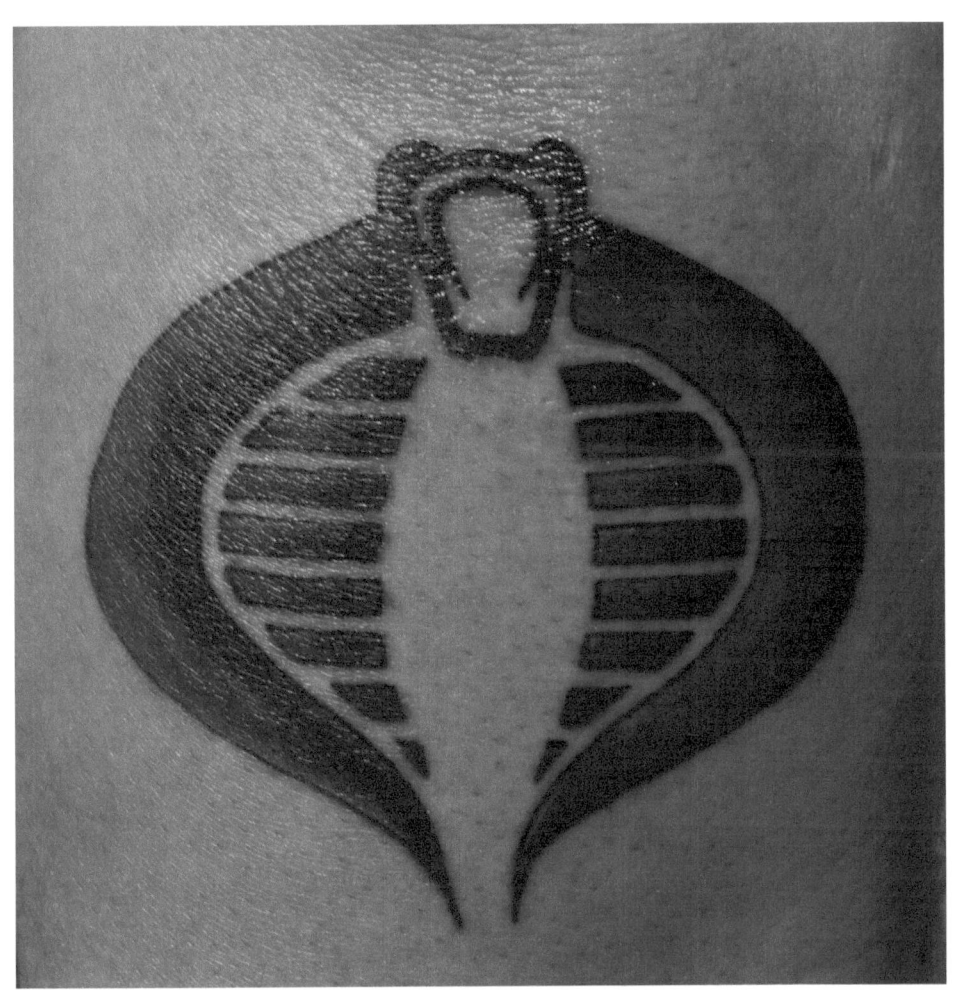

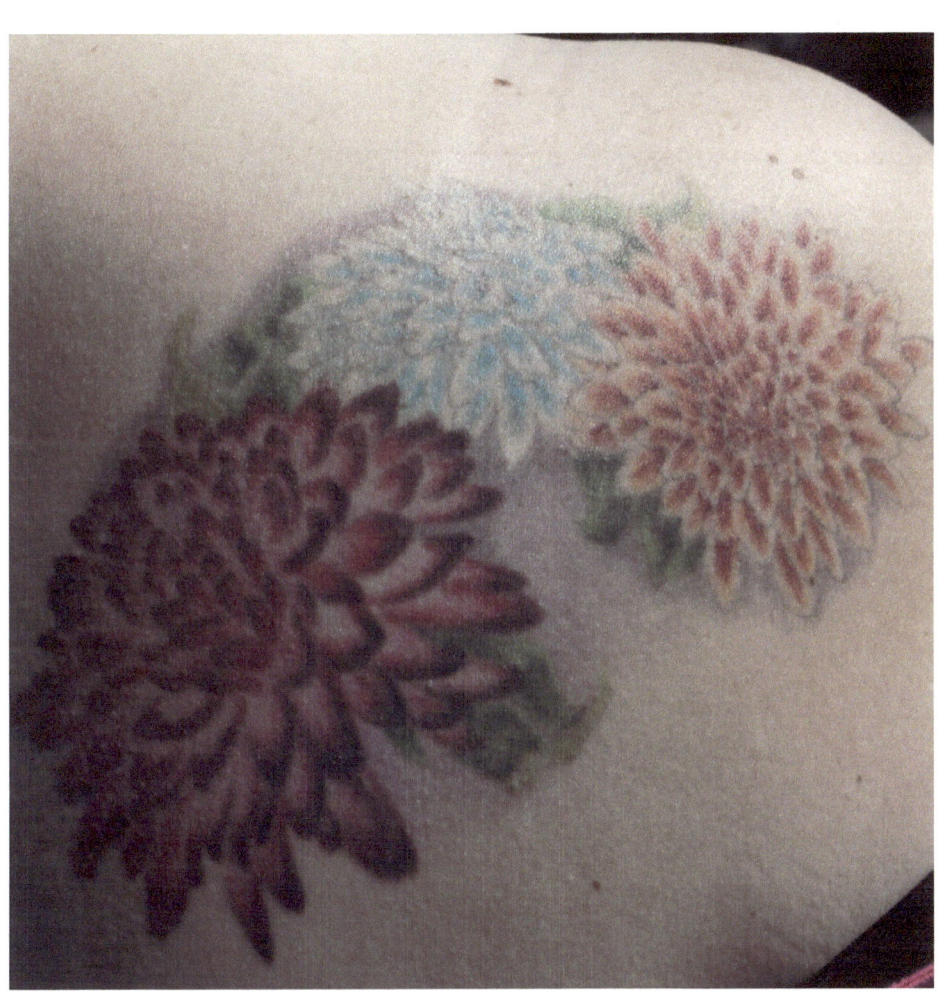

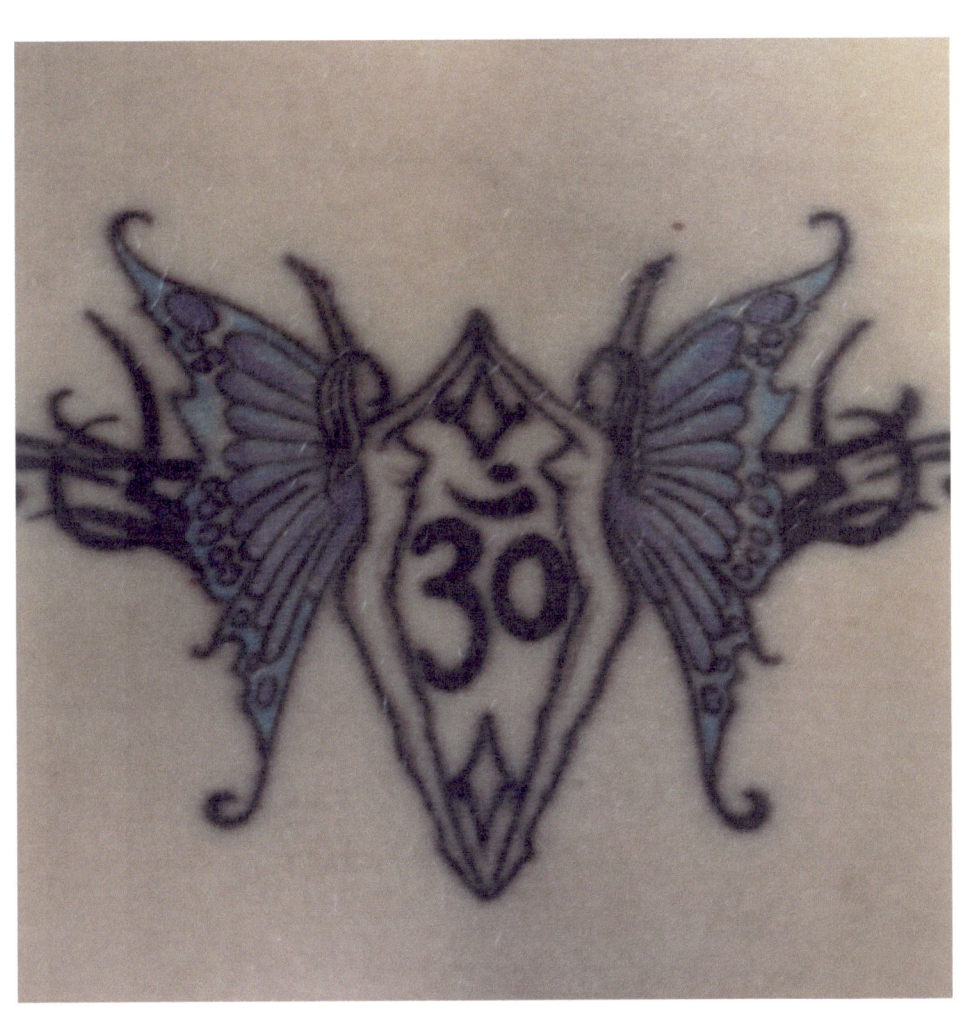

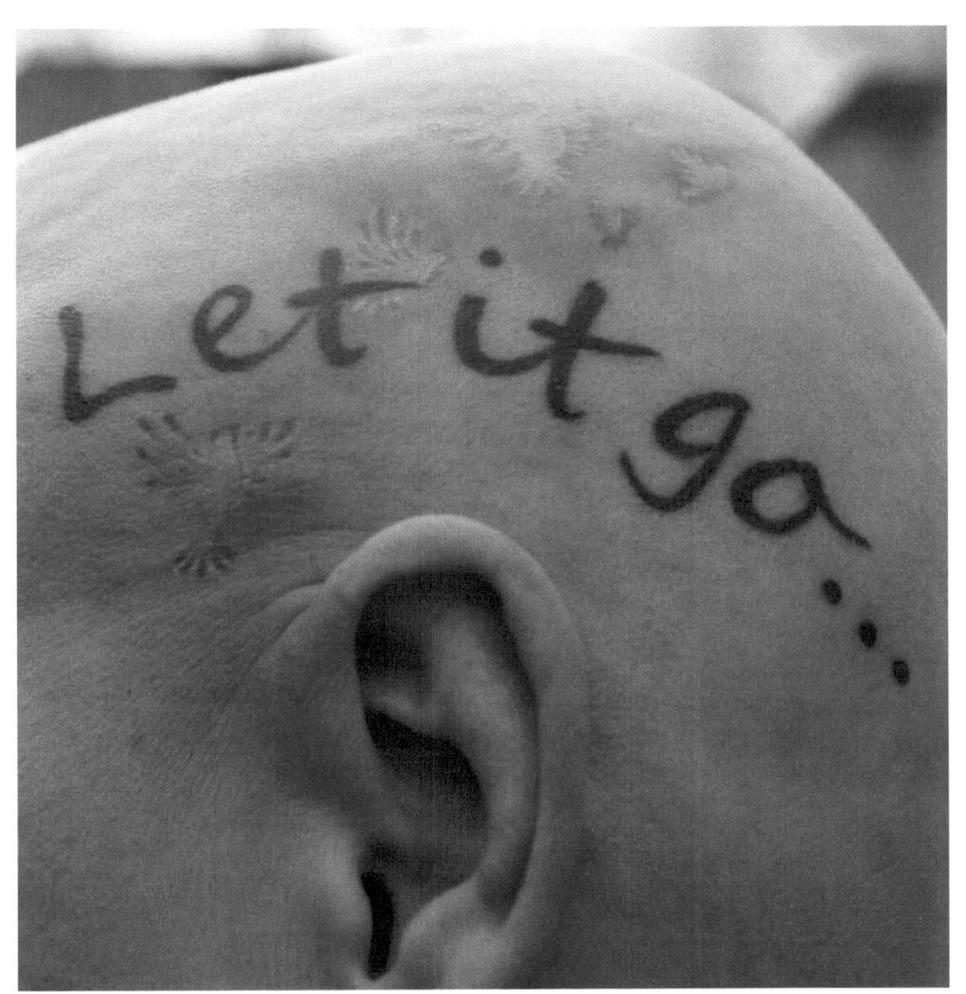

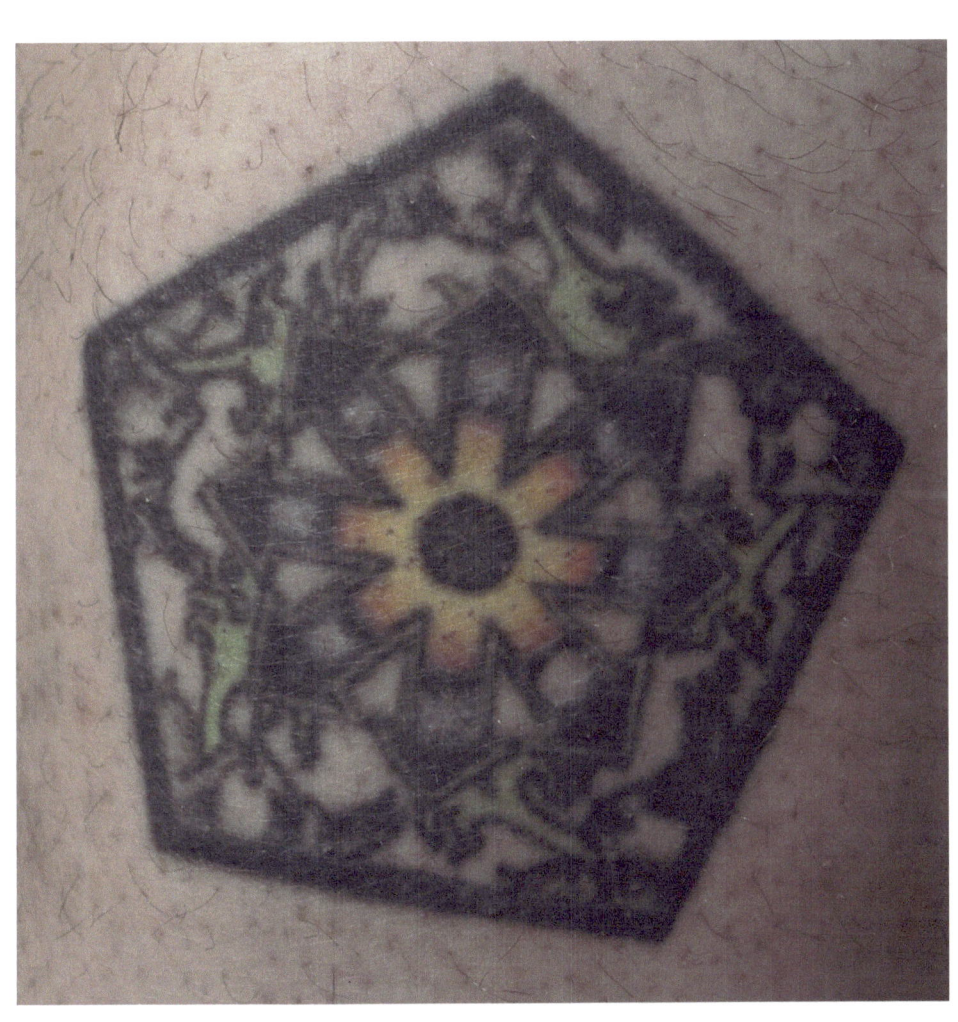

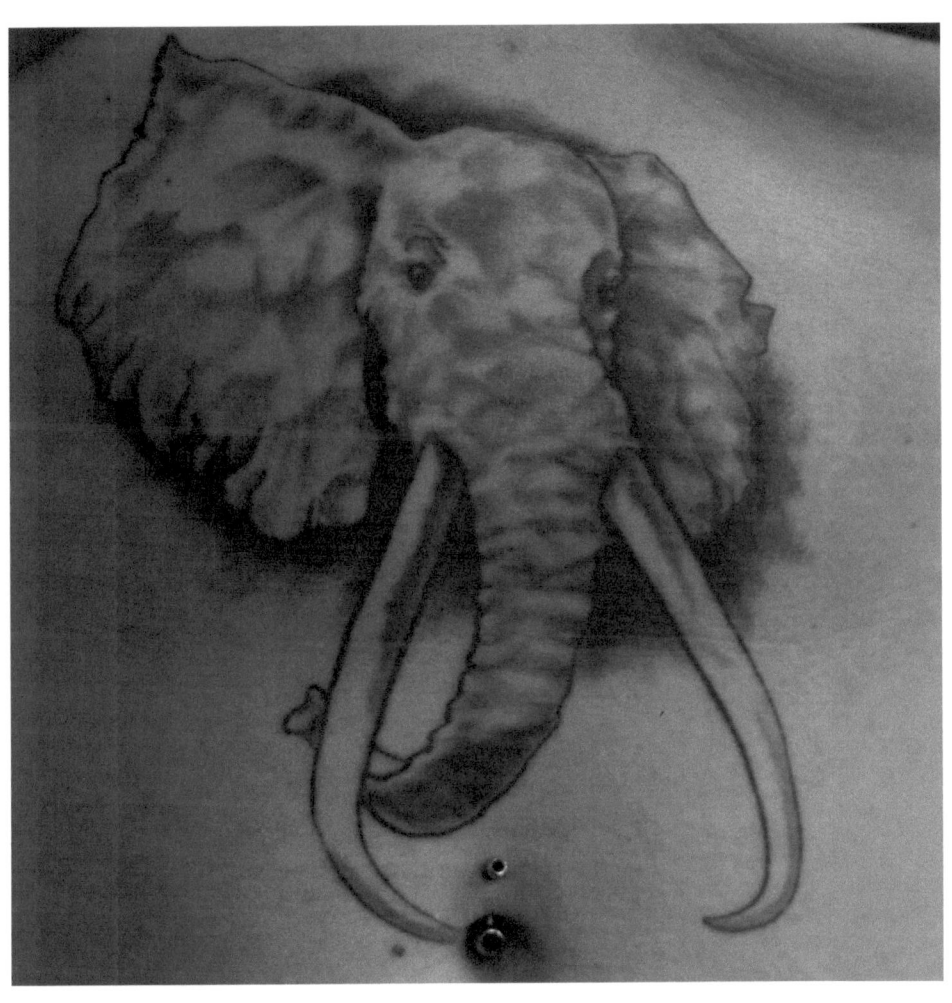

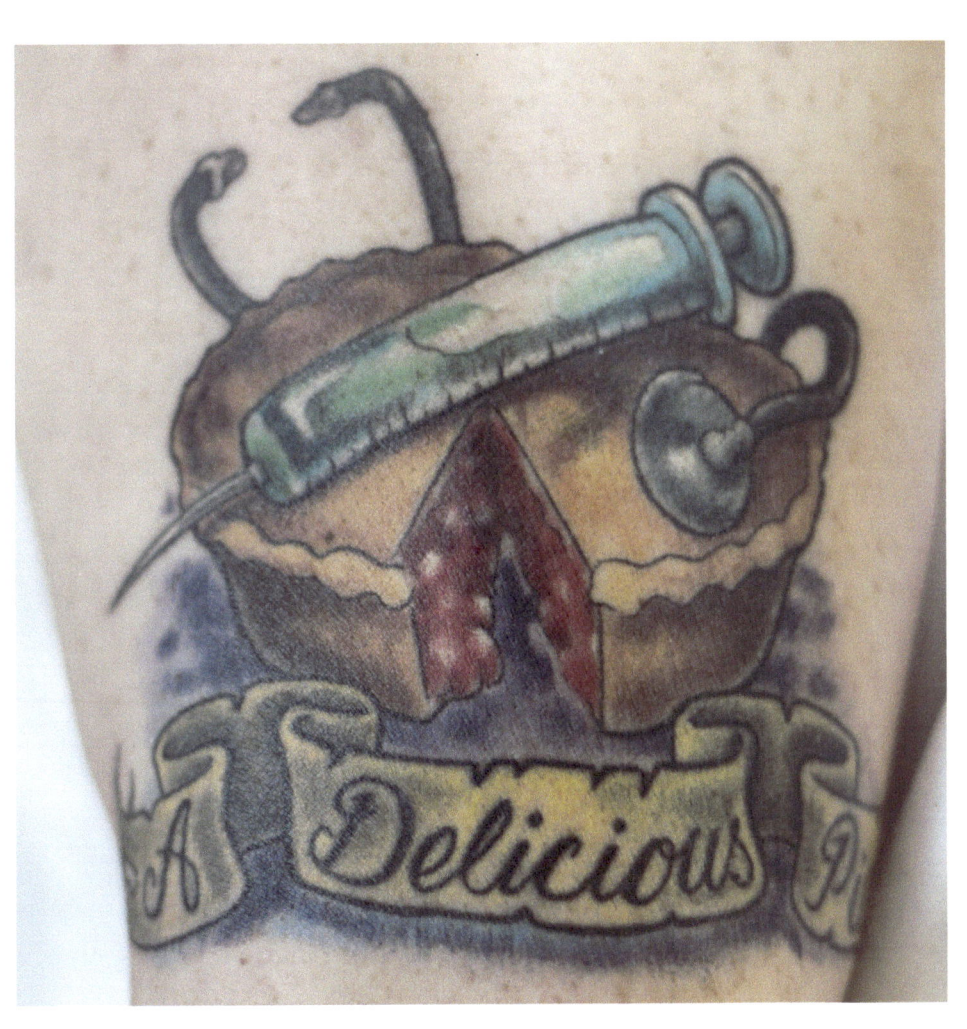

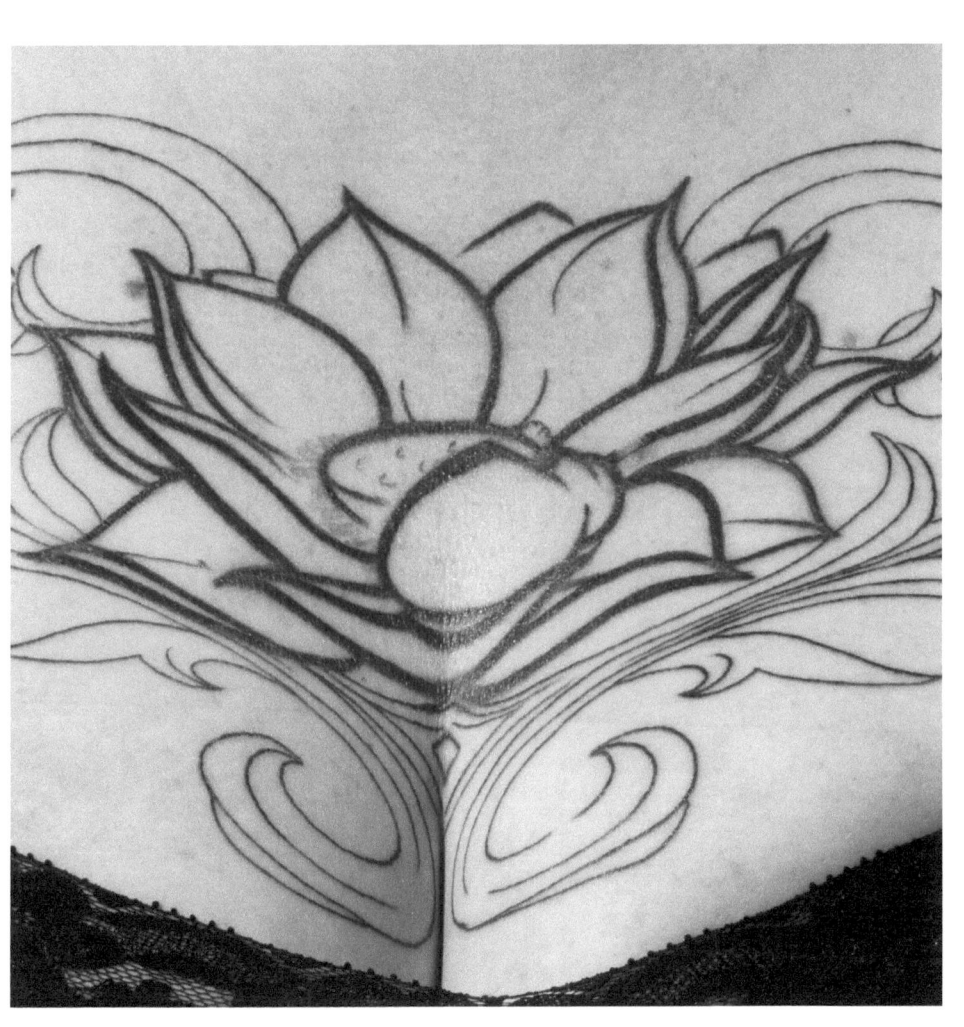

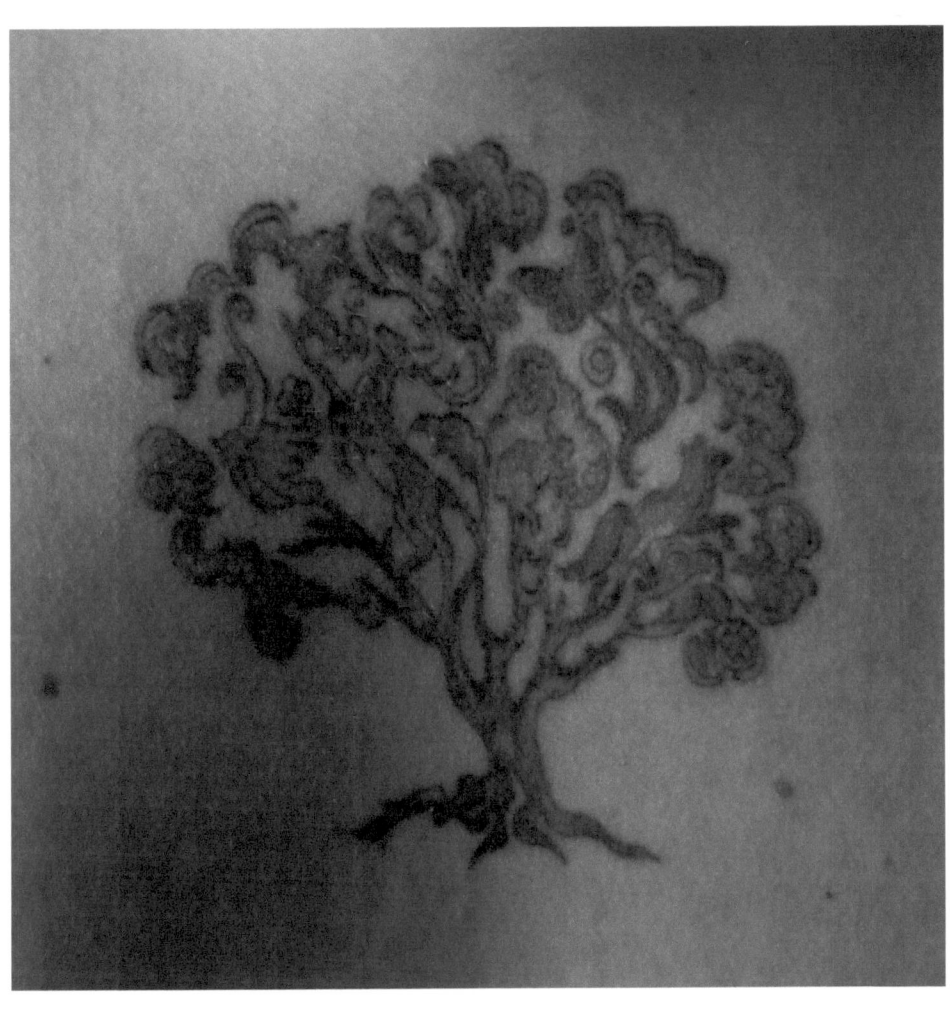

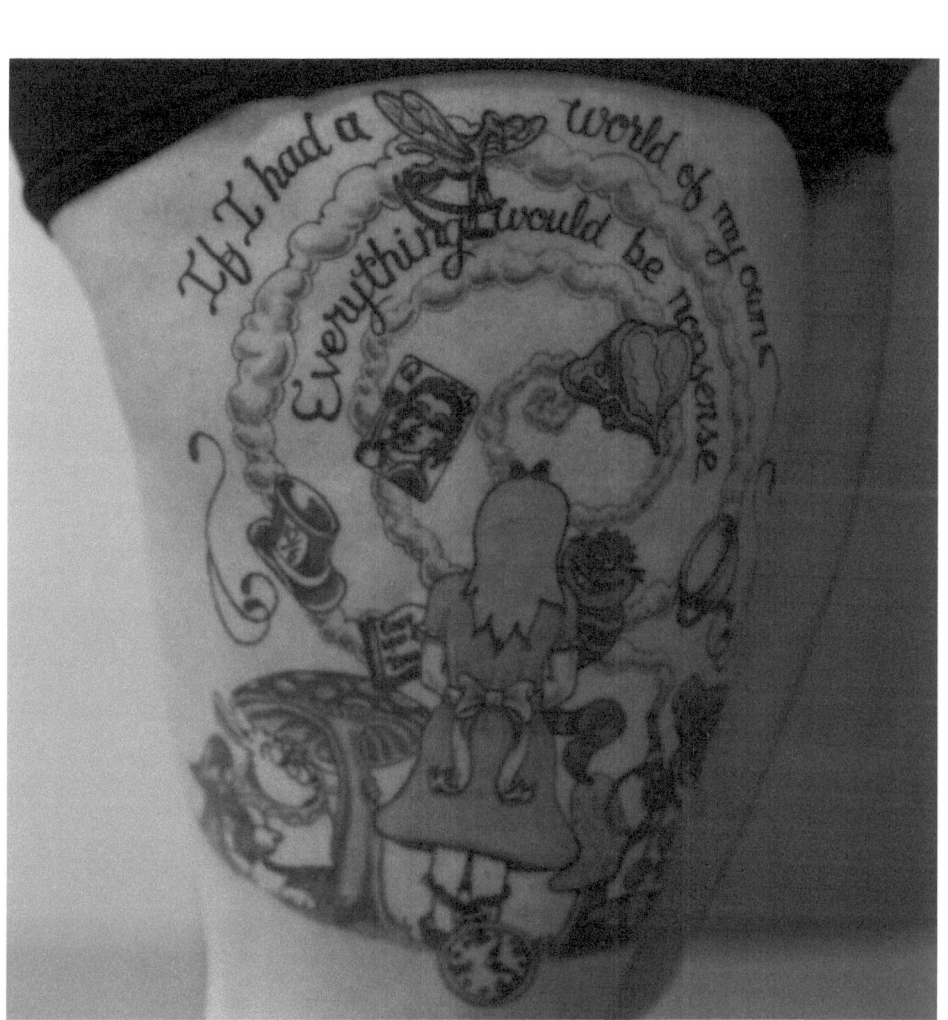

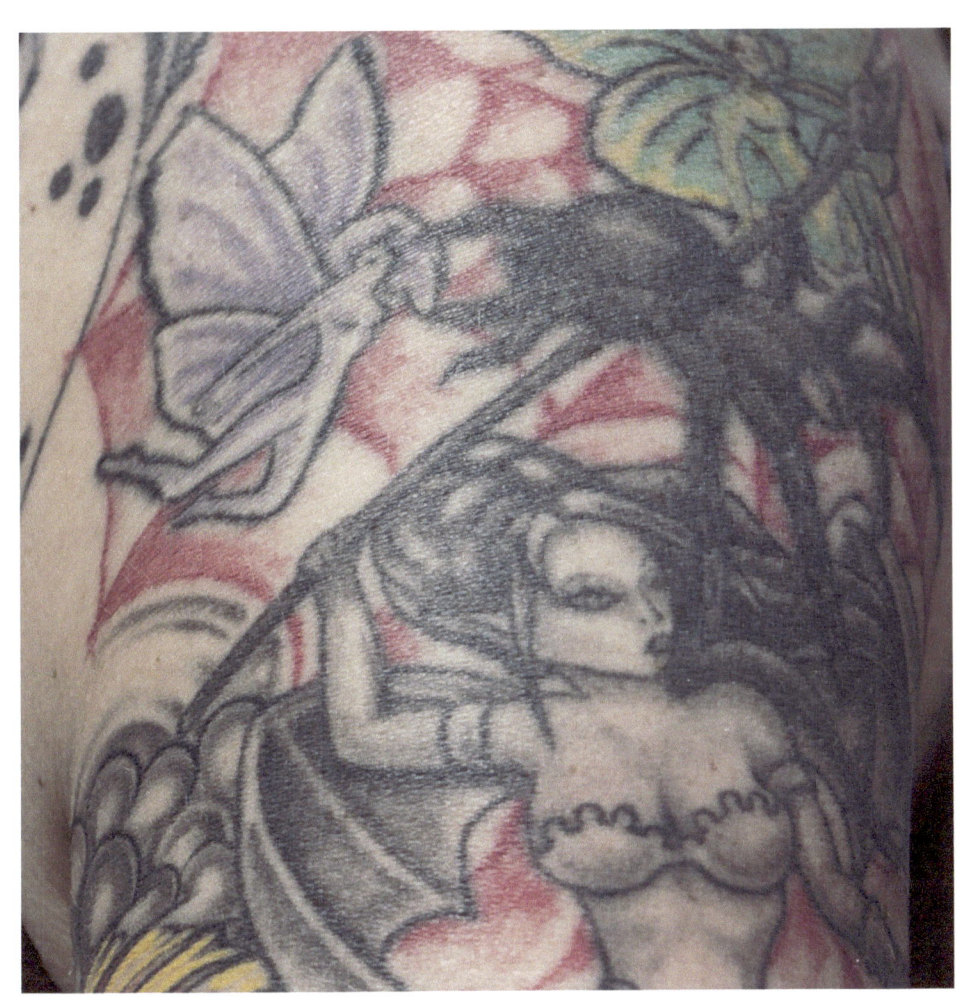

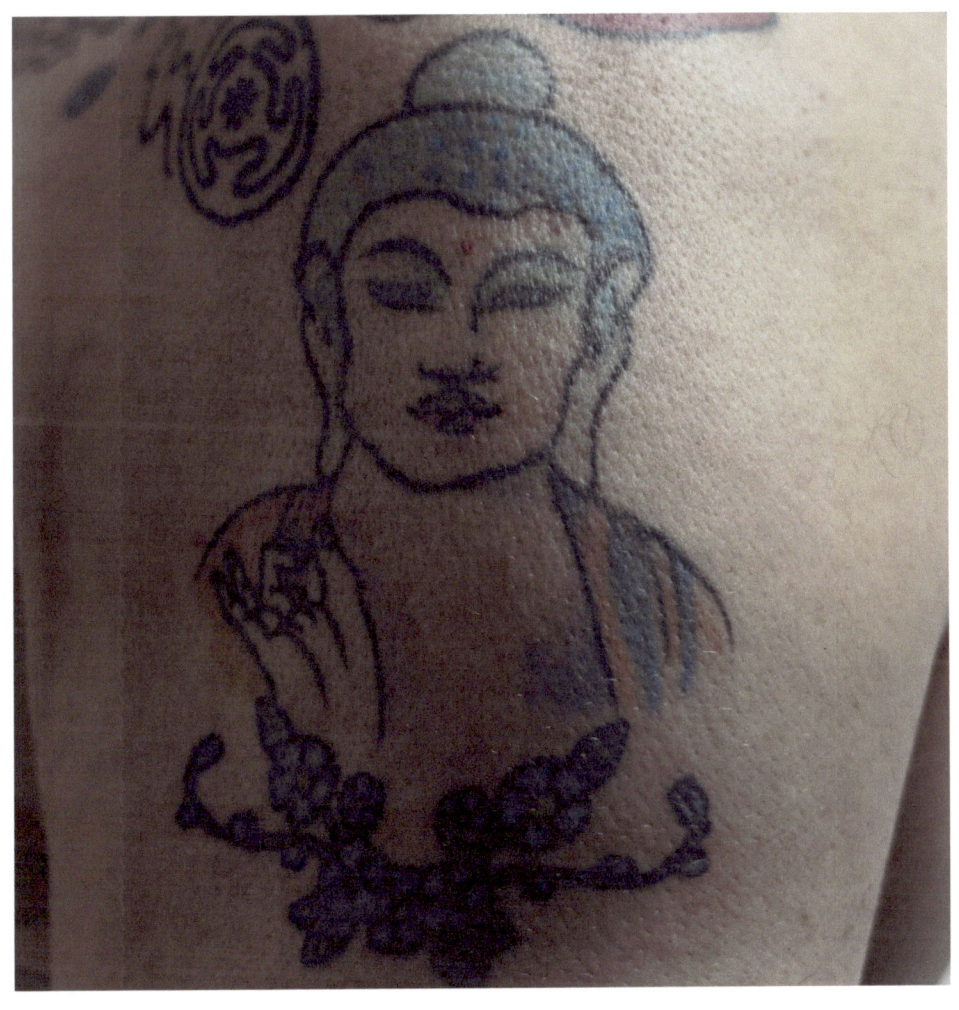

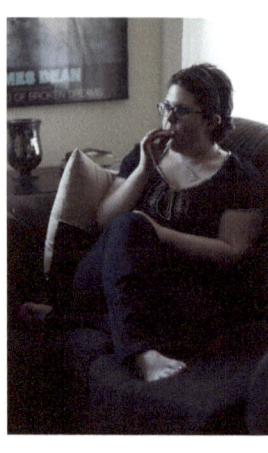
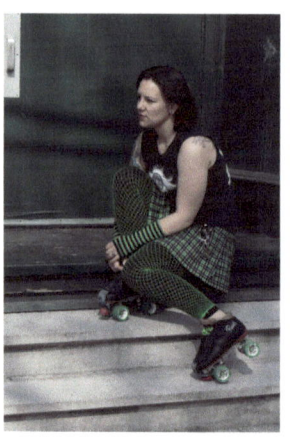
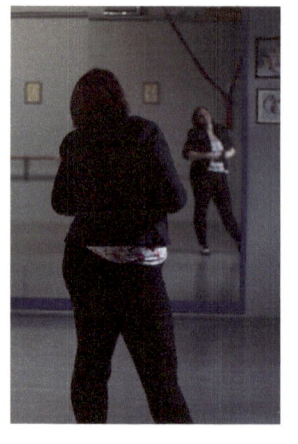
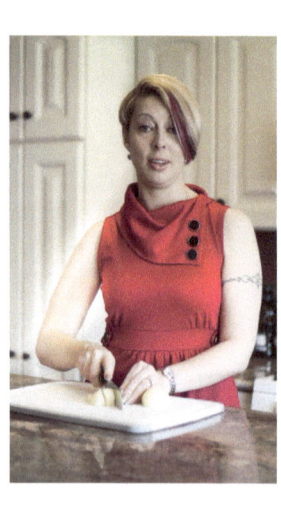
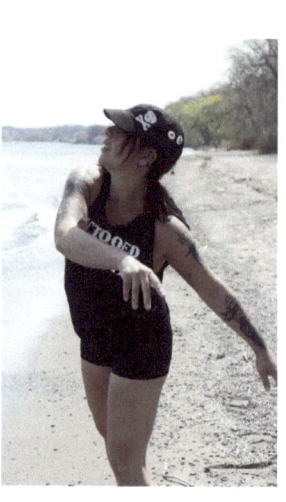
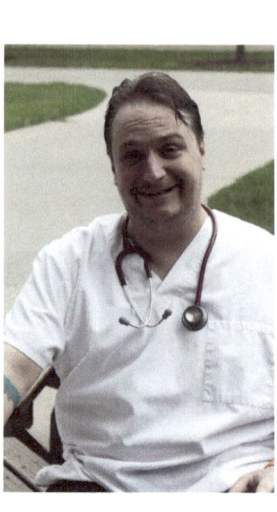
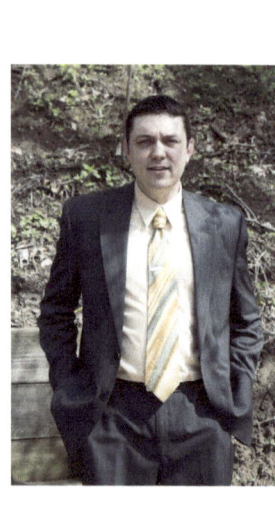
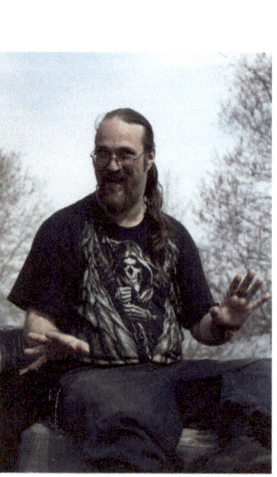
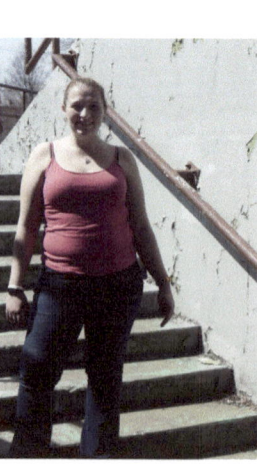

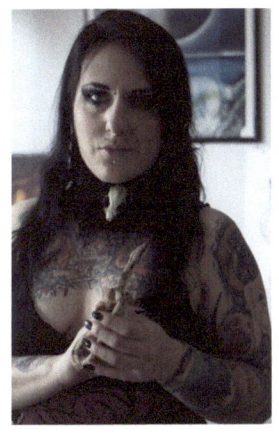 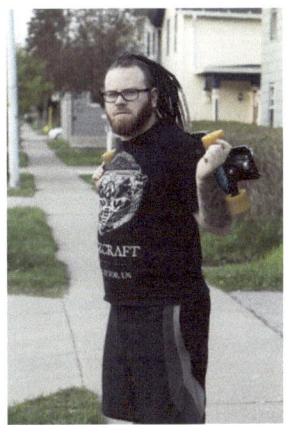 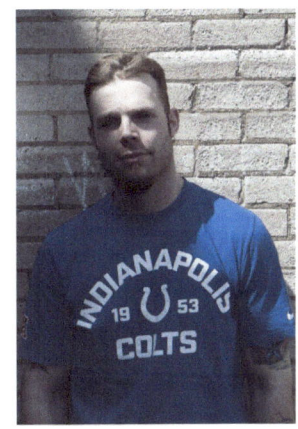

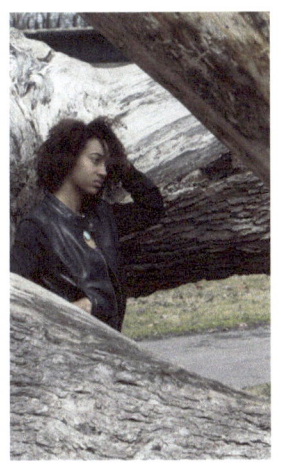 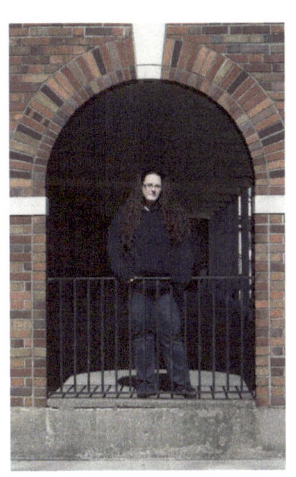 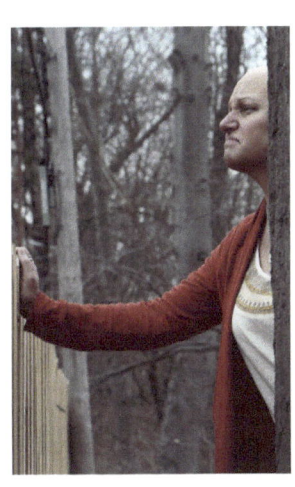

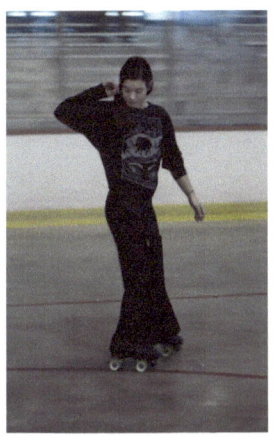 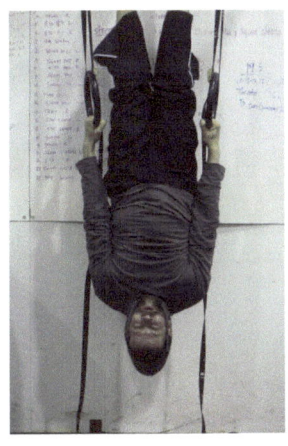

4,265 photos
17 people
5 weeks

This series was created as the final project for my Photo Arts II class at the Rochester Institute of Technology, during the Spring semester of 2014.

The series includes two types of photographs. First, a close-up image of the tattoo that each person chose as their favorite, or the one that best represents them. Secondly, there is an environmental portrait of each individual in a location of their choosing.

My hope is that you can't necessarily tell which tattoo belongs to which individual. Both types of "portrait" together show the diversity of tattooed people, and the set of people photographed.

A huge thank you to Voodoo Monkey Tattoo for putting me in contact with most of these wonderful people, and for tattooing a significant amount of artwork found on their skin.

Additional thanks especially to all of the beautiful individuals willing to be photographed and bear their tattooed skin for my camera lens.

This book was published two and a half years after the completion of the series, in the Fall of 2016.

www.ingramcontent.com/pod-product-compliance
Lightning Source LLC
Chambersburg PA
CBHW040818200526
45159CB00024B/3035